W9-BRE-416

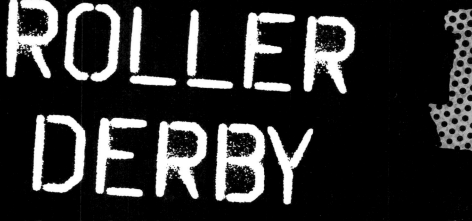

ROLLER DERBY

by Martha London

The **Greater** World of **Sports**

SportsZone

An Imprint of Abdo Publishing | abdobooks.com

abdobooks.com

Published by Abdo Publishing, a division of ABDO, PO Box 398166, Minneapolis, Minnesota 55439. Copyright © 2020 by Abdo Consulting Group, Inc. International copyrights reserved in all countries. No part of this book may be reproduced in any form without written permission from the publisher. SportsZone™ is a trademark and logo of Abdo Publishing.

Printed in the United States of America, North Mankato, Minnesota
092019
012020

THIS BOOK CONTAINS
RECYCLED MATERIALS

Cover Photos: Shutterstock Images, helmet, star; iStockphoto, roller skate
Interior Photos: John Paul Henry/The Paducah Sun/AP Photo, 5, AndyTullis/The Bulletin/AP Photo, 6; Ellen O'Nan/The Paducah Sun/AP Images, 7, 21; Sergei Bachlakov/Shutterstock Images, 8, 24; Bettmann/Getty Images, 11; Buyenlarge/Archive Photos/Getty Images, 12; George Skadding/The LIFE Premium Collection/Getty Images, 14; Daily News/NY Daily News Archive/Getty Images, 15; Rick Bowmer/AP Images, 17; Jon Super/AP Images, 19; Gregory Payan/AP Images, 20; Red Line Editorial, 23; Taylor Ballantyne/Sports Illustrated/Set Number: X162717 TK1/Getty Images, 27; Bart Ah You/Modesto Bee/AP Images, 29

Editor: Melissa York
Series Designer: Melissa Martin

Library of Congress Control Number: 2019941979

Publisher's Cataloging-in-Publication Data

Names: London, Martha, author
Title: Roller derby / by Martha London
Description: Minneapolis, Minnesota : Abdo Publishing, 2020 | Series: The greater world of sports | Includes online resources and index
Identifiers: ISBN 9781532190421 (lib. bdg.) | ISBN 9781532176272 (ebook)
Subjects: LCSH: Roller derby--Juvenile literature. | Roller skating--Juvenile literature. | Skaters--Juvenile literature. | Action sports (Extreme sports)--Juvenile literature. | Team games--Juvenile literature. | Sports--Juvenile literature.
Classification: DDC 796.21--dc23

TABLE OF CONTENTS

J
796.21
Lon

Chapter 1

TEAMMATES
ON WHEELS

During the week, girls from around the Seattle area gather in an empty warehouse. The smooth concrete floor makes it easy to skate. Paint lines mark out the track in the middle of the warehouse. In Seattle, roller derby isn't just for adults. Seattle Derby Brats is a youth league for girls ages 8 to 17.

The Galaxy Girls are practicing tonight. The team has won three consecutive national championships in junior league roller derby. The girls on this team practice skating a lot. They are all in their early teens. Some have been skating with Derby Brats for years.

Teamwork is key in roller derby.

Having the right gear keeps players safe and comfortable.

Everyone is dressed in comfortable clothes because it can get hot during practice. The girls wear knee pads, helmets, and mouth guards. Even in practice, safety is important.

During practice, the girls practice different formations. The coach suggests new strategies or other ideas. They practice many skills. One important skill that the skaters practice often is falling safely. They cross their arms over their chests. This helps cushion falls.

Falls are frequent during practice and matches.

All of the girls practice improving their speed and confidence in their skating. The jammers and the blockers work together. They are a team.

Roller derby is a full-contact sport. Women and men enjoy competing both in large tournaments and on small teams. Matches are fun to participate in and watch. But the best part about roller derby isn't the competition. The girls in the Seattle Derby Brats say they are more confident since joining the derby team. Roller derby is about having fun and finding your passion.

Players push and shove to get a good position during matches.

Chapter 2

THE START OF
ROLLER DERBY

Roller derby began in 1935. It was one of the first sports in which women competed with the same rules and regulations as men. That's because each team was a couple consisting of a woman and a man. Roller derby was not always structured the way it is today. Originally, it was a marathon sport.

Dancing, walking, and roller skating marathons date back to the 1880s. But in the 1930s, a sports event promoter put a new spin on skating. Leo Seltzer created events for the Chicago Coliseum in Chicago, Illinois, and he began a new event called the Transcontinental Roller Derby.

Roller skating became popular in the mid-1800s.

WES ARONSON

PEGGY O'NEAL

A postcard advertised roller derby and two famous skaters in 1940.

Seltzer designed a match with two-person teams skating 3,000 to 4,000 miles (4,800 to 6,400 km) around a track over the course of four or six weeks. A big map in the arena tracked each team's virtual progress across the United States.

The participants had to skate for 11.5 hours every day. One member from every team had to be skating around the banked track at all times.

The first 3,000-mile race had 25 teams skating. Thousands of people flocked to the arena every day to cheer on the skaters. Many of them didn't make it the whole month. Twisted ankles and exhaustion disqualified teams from continuing the race. Races like this first one were held in cities all over the country. Over time though, the sport began to evolve.

By 1937, roller derby had become a more physical and violent sport. New rules allowed skaters to touch, and teams won points for passing other teams. Soon skaters were shoving and trying to push other racers off the track. The crowd loved this kind of action. Because of this, roller derby changed how it was organized. Instead of two-person teams, two five-skater

Within a decade of its start, roller derby had evolved into a full-contact sport.

teams competed against each other. Matches were shorter and more action packed. Instead of racing to see who could skate 3,000 miles the fastest, now the goal was to see how fast a skater could move through a crowd and circle the track in a short amount of time.

Roller derby began to be televised in the 1940s. People enjoyed watching the sport at home. Throughout the 1960s, roller derby remained popular. During the TV era of roller derby, teams

Roller derby showcased fights and big personalities during the TV era.

were all women. However, by 1973, roller derby had lost a lot of its following. Matches were not aired on TV anymore. Some people tried to bring it back, but they were not successful.

WFTDA

The Women's Flat Track Derby Association (WFTDA) began first as the United Leagues Coalition (ULC) in 2004. At first, there were only a handful of teams. But over time, more and more derby teams started and joined the ULC. In 2006 the ULC became the Women's Flat Track Derby Association. Today, the WFTDA is the largest derby governing body in the world. Teams from all over the world are associated with the WFTDA.

In the early 2000s, a group of women in Texas began a flat-track league. Other leagues continued to skate on banked tracks. Today, roller derby continues to attract new athletes who are looking for a fun team sport to try.

Flat-track roller derby spread quickly around the country in the early 2000s.

Chapter 3

RULES OF ROLLER DERBY

Today, skaters don't have to be on their feet for 11.5 hours. Matches are much shorter, but they are fast paced. Each match is 60 minutes long, divided into two 30-minute halves. During each half, short periods called jams take place. Each jam lasts up to two minutes. At the end of the match, the team with the most points wins. If there is a tie, an overtime jam will occur to break the tie.

Roller derby teams can have many players. However, during a jam, only five players can be on the track. Players include the jammers, blockers, and pivots, who are a special type of blocker.

Each position has a specific role to play during the jam.

The jammer's helmet has a star on it so the player is easy to identify.

Jammers are the offensive players. They are the only skaters who can score points. Once a jammer completes a lap around the track, she starts getting points. The number of points she scores depends on how many of the opponent's blockers she passed in her lap. A jammer who gets ahead of the blockers early might get as many as four points—one for each blocker. But more often, blockers stick close to the jammer so she may only get one or two points for each lap.

Blockers and pivots are the team's defense. Their job is to keep the other team's jammer from passing them. A pivot is a type of blocker. But she is a leader on the team. She is a play-caller. It is the pivot's job to set up a play that blocks the opponent's jammer while still allowing her own jammer through. Blockers stay close together in a pack. The pack makes it difficult for the jammer to

Blockers and pivots try to keep back the other team's players.

pass. As jammers and blockers fight for position, the skaters push each other to attempt to knock the other team members off balance and open a hole in the pack for the jammer to get through. This is what makes roller derby a contact sport.

The Jammer Star

Jammers are recognized by the star on their helmet. The star is on a stretchy piece of fabric that goes over the jammer's helmet. In the pack, it can be difficult to tell who is pushing and who needs blocking. The star signals to all players who the scorers are. If something happens to the jammer, the pivot can take over the jammer's star. Doing this is called a star pass.

Skaters use quad skates that have four wheels and rubber toe-stops. The toe-stops allow skaters to stop or slow down quickly. The skaters also use them to push off from the floor and gain speed.

Players wear knee pads, helmets, mouth guards, elbow guards, and wrist guards. This gear

ROLLER DERBY TRACK

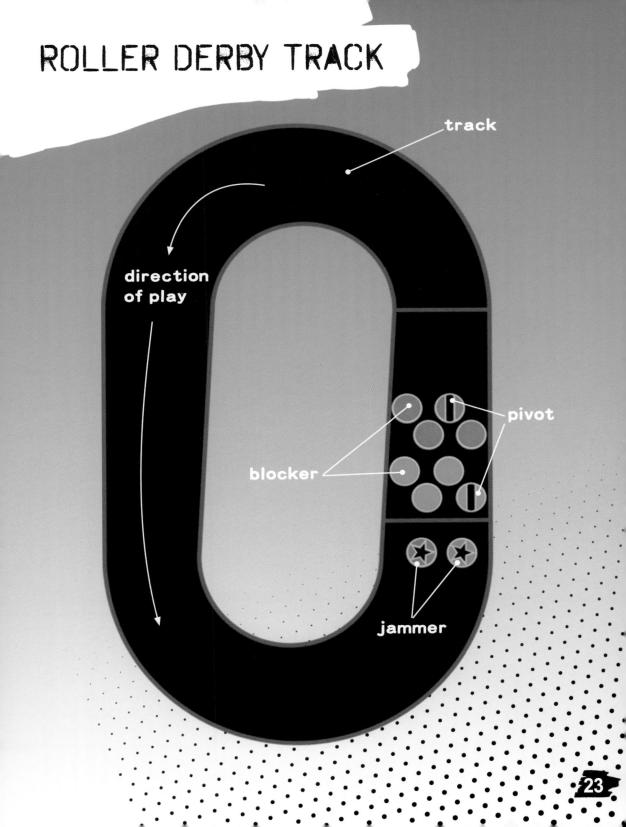

track

direction
of play

pivot

blocker

jammer

protects players when they are pushed and fall to the concrete floor. It is not uncommon for skaters to run into each other and land on the floor in a pile. Having gear that protects the skaters from injury is important.

Even with helmets and pads in place, injuries still occur. The most common types include knee and ankle injuries. Head injuries like concussions are also common.

Gear prevents some injuries, but not all.

Chapter 4

ROLLER DERBY
LEAGUES

Roller derby teams compete all over the world. One of the largest governing bodies for roller derby is the Women's Flat Track Derby Association (WFTDA). More than 450 leagues across six continents belong to the WFTDA. Teams that are a part of the WFTDA play in international games. The WFTDA holds a regular season and then playoffs. The top four teams get automatic invitations to the championships. The next 24 teams compete in the International Playoffs to play in the championships.

Teams that are not ranked high enough to compete in the International Playoffs are seeded

Manhattan Mayhem is one of four teams in New York's Gotham Girls league, one of the founding members of WFTDA.

into regional playoffs in North America and Europe. This guarantees that almost all derby teams are able to compete in the same number of regular-season and playoff-season games.

The Men's Roller Derby Association (MRDA) hosts tournaments for men's derby teams. When roller derby was first created, men and women played together, but over time, derby became associated with women. Men's roller derby is growing in popularity. It doesn't have as many participants as women's, but that may be changing as junior derby leagues attract more kids, regardless of gender. However, coed teams are rare.

Beyond the Track

Many roller derby leagues also hold charity matches that raise funds for local or state nonprofit organizations. For example, Maine Roller Derby holds the Thanks-For-Giving fundraiser every November. Audience members and officials can join in the jams, and they hold dance parties on the track.

Some junior leagues have coed teams for kids of any gender.

Small community teams and teams associated with college clubs may play against WFTDA or MRDA teams, but they do not qualify for larger WFTDA or MRDA events. But for many teams, that is okay because the point of roller derby isn't to win a big trophy. It's about building community and having a good time.

GLOSSARY

banked

Having slanted sides like the sides of a bowl.

concussion

A bad injury to the brain that causes short-term brain malfunctions.

consecutive

Occurring in a row.

flat track

A track that does not have slanted sides.

international

Across the world.

regional

Within a contained area like a state or part of a country.

seeded

Ranked according to how many matches a team won.

MORE INFORMATION

BOOKS

Graham, Felicia. *Rollergirls: The Story of Flat Track Derby*. San Antonio, TX: Trinity University Press, 2018.

London, Martha. *Quidditch*. Minneapolis, MN: Abdo Publishing, 2020.

Parnavelas, Ellen. *The Roller Derby Athlete*. London, UK: Bloomsbury, 2012.

ONLINE RESOURCES

To learn more about roller derby, please visit **abdobooklinks.com** or scan this QR code. These links are routinely monitored and updated to provide the most current information available.

INDEX

ABOUT THE AUTHOR

Martha London writes books for young readers full time. When she isn't writing, you can find her hiking in the woods.